patmos

patmos

poems

BRUCE BOND

UNIVERSITY OF MASSACHUSETTS PRESS
Amherst and Boston

Printed in the United States of America

ISBN 978-1-62534-561-5 (paper)

Designed by Sally Nichols
Set in Marion
Printed and bound by Integrated Books International

Cover design by adam bohannon
Cover art by Carl Dobsky, *Maggie and the Satellites,* 2013.
Used with permission.

Library of Congress Cataloging-in-Publication Data
A catalog record for this book is available from the Library of Congress.

British Library Cataloguing-in-Publication Data
A catalog record for this book is available from the British Library.

These perfect and private things, walling us in, have imperfect and public endings—
Water and wind and flight, remembered words and the act of love
Are but interruptions. And the world, like a beast, impatient and quick,
Waits only for those who are dead. No death for you. You are involved.

—Weldon Kees, "The Smiles of the Bathers"

contents

patmos

The radio at the end of time is playing a song in a room alone.
It is a New Year's favorite about forgetting or not in the form
of a question. All these years have ended with a question.
All these questions with a room alone. I have had that dream.
And the sirens and smoke of the holy land scratched words
against a sky that ate them. And we all sang together, because
why not. Music brings a stranger closer. It is how, these many
years, we survived. In our rooms, alone, at the end of time.

Pages fall, wave over wave, and still the modern ocean
swells, every continent an island, every island small.
An eye shines with acid rain, and the blinding of the news
is hopeless. *No end to interpretation,* my friend said,
and he passed in his sleep like a reader-response theory
eaten by a tabloid. The headline reads, there is no end.
No place where poison drinks the word *poison* and dies.
No page that gives the light of the planet a place to fall.

However old the language, it is not dead. It is the child
in the doll, the Christ in a wafer, the ocean in the sleep
machine that turns slowly back to water. Say the word
salt, and it clarifies against you. I learned that from the sea
that gave us life. It gave us the word *soul,* from the Proto-
German *saiwaz,* the path souls travel before the world
and after. And when you speak, you feel their passing.
You hear them step across the phosphor and the hiss.

At the end of a phrase played with inquisitive touch,
with the tenderness that attention breeds, time swells.
Everything returns to nothing, and the nothing knows:
to write a better closure you need a bit of the future,
a lot of the lost. You need a friend's coffin to rise
at the end of a novel you read slow, and read again.
This will be your lifeboat, your avatar's last hope,
borne up from the wreck that has no other answer.

Cheerful stories frighten me, the ones that say, go ahead,
lift all the sanctions. The sea will swallow all that ails you.
It will take your refusals, your shipwrecks, your refugees,
your sludge and poison bled from factories of the shore.
It was made for this, for mornings after, the shame of them,
the shamelessness to come. Every morning, the sea will
sob against your door. But rest assured. It will leave you.
It will leave at your mat the weeds and refuse of the deep.

No end to interpretation, my friend said, and then,
he died. *Passed on,* said his brother at the service.
I too avoided the word that had in it so little room
or far too much. What do I know of a thing that is
all too certain. *Words have no other side,* my friend
would say. He says it still, and I ask, do we dream
in obscurities to protect the mind, or to create it.
For the ones you lost, what language would you choose.

What the end of this tune needs is a silence to accept it.
It needs a box marked *handle with care,* and a voice to say,
here, without saying it precisely. Today I felt the first snow
falling in my hair. I felt a younger self step out of my body
beneath the dark towers of the pines. And together we stared
into the fire, transfixed. Whatever our burden, the light would
bring us closer. Light devoured light. Grief, grief. Whosever
ashes these, they feathered upward into heaven. With the snow.

If I was the rope, she was the bell, and together we would toll
until the bronze fell back in its tower, but the flash and stutter
traveled on, and I could hear, as she laid her head beside me,
flushed and breathing, a siren in the distance, the rise and fall
into a silent chamber. In truth, only the idea of it was silent,
only its proximity to noise. The world is always larger than it is.
And smaller. Ask the fly at the window, the bored child,
the steeple's needle, the bell. Just like a fly to fall for a window.

Whenever arrival would justify the journey, I am lost,
free to make a better story, a better end. And I know
someday a wind will blow the sand-mandala of our planet.
The sea will lift into the sky and take with it its mirror.
But I will cherish my diminished repertoire of choices.
I will write the future, dear love, I miss you, and a long
night will settle over the paper. I will stare into whatever
light remains, somewhere in the middle we call an end.

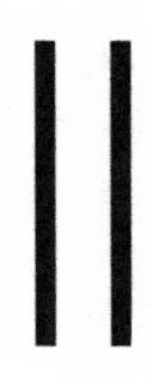

Once there was a mother who took her children each
Sunday to the sea and never swam. Her hair was perfect.
As time is when it stiffens, or a heaven without animals.
An ocean turns breathless, and so you walk across.
Perfect, from the old French *parfit,* for completed.
A good life is full of endings, and you can find them
in the small and beautiful boxes at the foot of her bed.
You can open and close and open forever, like the tide.

As a child, I read the sky at night. It was full of nothing
and fires nailed to nothingness, so long as I could see.
Light archival and wordless still. And I was headed there,
beyond the bear, the twin, the stories told to children in
the woods. I felt nervous, boundless, awed. The world
beyond constellation took on the shade of black known
only to interior spaces. Call it faith. Or utter lack of faith.
I, a child, did not know the difference. I am a child still.

When a father leaves, the sea becomes a sky laid low.
On a far horizon, the *incognitas* of the ancient world.
And you sail toward the edge where the water pours.
When a father dies, the earth's edge is a cataract of stars.
Why the ocean never empties is anyone's guess.
But if you look hard, you might see a blur on the floor.
If you lean over the water, you see a body, a face,
beneath the fathoms, pinned by starlight to the eye.

When I was young, my Lord was clear as consciousness.
And so he slipped in and out of our ears, our mouths.
He was a part of each, the sum of every, of time no less,
its body and its angel, and so I named him *the long view*
for whom we have no name. Bewildering, as music is,
as I watched my father open a book of hymns and sing
of a god he never spoke of, his breath drawn through a place
I never knew. But from the distance of a song, I heard.

I live so close to the funeral home, I hear the sad favorites
on the Hammond organ. The music for one voice or none.
The glass of the heart wrapped in cotton. The silence that so
misses its twin, you can hear them as one and never know.
There is a mercy in that. The minimal grace of bewildered spaces.
Every Sunday, the black limousine gets soaped and polished.
I have watched them with their rags without knowing I am
watching. The jewel of the neighborhood, its headlights burning.

If, as you leave the scene of the accident, you feel heavy-
limbed, light-headed, more than shattered, less than numb,
take heart. The crumpled hood huffing steam on the cliff
will be your angel. It will stare transfixed across the guardrail.
Wind will lean into your ear and whisper, *a body in motion
stays in motion.* And the road from here will be more deadly
and sublime. You will lie back down in the snow and wait
for the pain to arrive, for the medic's light to search your eyes.

My father looked all night for the story of his bloodline.
It gave him a consolation of ghosts in the shapes of trees.
Every branch a mother, every leaf a child among the others
beneath a tree. Heaven was an earth, and earth the sum
total of every dawn. And so it never died. We planted
a tree in his memory. It is larger now, though the plaque
with his name on it is smaller. Every fall, the leaves drift over,
scatter. Every time I kneel to read, the leaves fall through.

I felt compelled to choose, to pledge allegiance to the wall.
I was told, fear God because he loved me. Love my father,
and so I felt afraid. Death was a small object in the distance.
Like me, beneath a desk. Looking down at the floor, I felt
compelled to choose. Earth or life on the surface. I know.
I would always have a name, a small object in the distance.
But who survives to read it. When the missiles fall, who will
ask the question. Where does heaven go when heaven dies.

If not heaven, why not this. Why not paradise as the meal
between us, the story you are telling, how you and I would make
it mine. Why not the night your father carried you, asleep,
from the Hollywood Bowl to the car. Or was that your dream
on the long ride home. It's all talk now, and the deeper we go,
the more the talk gets quiet, small, as if, with eyes of the sleepless,
we are entering the bedroom of a child, and you say, I buried
my father in his works on earth. And I whisper, me too, me too.

I was just another creature crawling from the mausoleum,
and I thought, so this is it, the place in the final chapter
where I'm judged for my cruelties, blunders, failures of attention,
and I waited for the furies to take me, or some such host.
But it was just another morning. My mother was asleep
and would not wake again. *I am here,* I said. I say it still,
whenever I am back there, sleeping, as words are when you
love them, when you read them to a woman who is gone.

The end of the world goes largely unrecorded, but it
was always there. Always those poor souls among us
who had that dream last night. You see it in their bodies,
the way they hold back whatever flood or nuclear winter.
You too could go cold and never see the ship go under.
You could awaken in a stiffer posture, bewildered, if not
broken, and never know what it is that holds you, stuns you,
your curtains lit and unlit with the passage of the clouds.

You wake, you rise. In the style of mourners and bells
and modern oceans, you overfill your borders. You open
a door and, in your leaving, enter a sea that is everywhere
the air we breathe and so in every age. Wherever you go,
the story of the end keeps wafting back from a distant place,
the words blurred, rhapsodic, if eroded, but here you are,
free to move, to hear in the long strides of the breeze whatever
you most fear and desire, where your need to speak begins.

And then your curtains burn a little brighter. They sigh
the visual sigh of dusk at dawn, and your heart floats back
into its chamber. Is there solace knowing the end is over.
Has the torrent torn a passage. Do you emerge an infant
bathed in the wreckage of your journey, having seen what
the dead see who return afraid and will not tell their tale.
Do you say, *at least that's over,* and find your refuge, here,
where waters rise and rise each night to tar the morning shore.

It must bring comfort to a few, these confessionals online.
Upload your worry, and watch it float from the grave of one
more night, your face in the liquid crystal that casts no shade.
Mostly our sins are ordinary and make us feel a little criminal.
And like children, a little special. Online everyone is as special
as stone. Not to say our missteps are benign. We could walk
the narrow path, undistracted by the damned, the meth teeth
and whores who burn. We could be as criminal as angels.

You never know. The odd survivor with ashes in her hair
could sit across your table. Is there something you want
to ask or say, that she is not alone. Surely, we have all
suffered enough. Do you agree. Do you say *we* or *you*
when what you mean is *I am here to talk, if you are haunted,*
hunted, broken or confused, a stranger to the others.
Does the woman at the community table look up
from her phone to say, *What the hell are you looking at.*

Say you find yourself among the wretched swept
into a pit of burning hair. I have studied scripture
by a light like this. I have read the stories of the few
who die and go to hell, and back, and what they feel
is not guilt. But shame. No absolution. No cure.
Any wonder we have heard so little about it. Always
the great white light. But for the damned on earth,
whom do they trust to cut them open, sew them up.

Suicidal cults give their children to Jesus. The world
is not their world anymore. It is a text. Angels come
in their spaceships to repossess the faithful, harvest them
for a star untouched by hands. What good are hands
when everything has happened. Do not weep, they say,
for those you love. They love you and are strangers still.
They will not hear you, hold you. They stare at names
in stone to read, as lovers do, far too little. And then, too much.

The voices on the radio are calling in from the heartland,
crossing over into static and back, looking for an ear to lie
down in, to be the grave of loneliness, bitterness, graves.
The world is not their world any more. It is a story that ends,
over and over, with an angry Sabbath or talk show host.
Heaven waits, as the lambs of the new age wait. The end,
they hear, is the finest part. They hear and so they follow.
They drink their death. And take a little extra for the pain.

IV

John of Patmos lived on an island, and who in the age
of broken trust does not. Moonlight beats the shattered
beach, and it must have been lonely, waiting for God,
for the curve of the horizon to send a horse. If, beneath
the sun, a mirage across the water gave birth to lions,
any wonder the sea rose, the island dwindled. Longing
for news like a soul for a body, one body for a mate,
any wonder he saw the shoreline eaten by the waves.

Those nights I kept vigil beside my mother, her eyes
opened, now and then. If she was there, I could not tell,
her gaze so thin, like a paper cut. Sometimes a yawn.
Sometimes a lion of the apocalypse, only smaller,
fiercer. What if it is nothing, she asked. What was I
to say, I who believed in something better for her sake.
And as I walked in darkness to my car, I smelled something
burning. Leaves, I thought, and wind gone out to meet them.

My worry makes me taller, more fatherly, suspicious
of pride and thereby prouder, so who am I to say, I
worry about John. If he ate crickets and watercress
and slept an hour, here and there, doubtless he longed
to be a better man. But when he emerged, bearing news,
I wonder, did the casualties of men make him a better
listener. He must have felt the blister of all that fire, his
personal hell, I say, and who am I, I wonder. Who.

I have been that child in the fire, and the beams of houses
toppled to earth. Graves exhaled their dead like gasoline.
Lost, divided, looking for my wife, I kept running into walls,
calling her name. Windows covered their eyes and melted.
I should tell you. My wife was just then waking to the terrors
of her childhood. She found them in a place like this.
She stared them down. Call this dream a good dream, then.
All dreams are. The wounded mind is lonely for the mind.

One wall lies against another, but it is never the same wall.
Never the same dull beat of the bed on the other side.
The child body you lived in once—its bruises belonged
to a child. If you think you are alone, imagine her. Say
you are at the table again, head bowed to what you cannot,
will not, eat. And you know your mom worked hard.
She tells you. You feel guilty, if not a bit empowered.
You pity the meat, how it died for you. And will not rise.

The lonely call-in radio host sharpens his tongue
against the silence, *and another thing,* he says to no
one there, phones dark, doors closed, in the corner
a rubric written in light: *on air. The Jews own everything*
these days, he says. Then, a call. And then, another.
No sooner *Jew* is every other word and leaps, phone
to phone, across the switchboard, come to storm heaven
and hell. It fills the air with fire and angels. It's everywhere.

After the bombs to end all bombs descend, an angel,
blown back-first toward the end of time, looks this way,
and, as the present moment moves, so too the angel,
as if a paradise were always falling. That is its nature.
Even now as we sit together in the sands of Nevada,
and the blast in the distance razes another makeshift
homestead at dawn. The sublimity so old in us it feels
like the future. Like a child's child. And we, her angel.

The end is unconscious the moment it arrives. Every decade,
the apocalypse comes. It goes. Some are changed, or feel
changed, some cast out, weary as meat, and a lioness appears.
In a better dream, my body sees its end in every other. I call
my wife's name into a tower on fire. I do not think I save her.
I do not know if she saves me. But as I wake, I shout. I walk
into the door weeping from its hinges. And it goes on and on.
My calling. Hers. The smoldering enclosure, the ax of dawn.

Wherever you are wounded, you are not quite there,
not quite yourself thrashing a shore that will not give,
searching for those you lost and, on your knees, must
lose again. Just like a sea to try to pound the terror out.
But come dawn, it will be you who survives, and you will
hear your loved ones passing in the waves, breathing in
the pale narcosis of the fog. *No need,* they will whisper,
to break your sternum open. The world has nightmares of its own.

The one hand clapping at the end of the long dark hall
is a friend of mine. Every time I think I am alone, I hear
the severed hand walk back from an enormous distance.
If music could talk it would say, distance is nothing to me.
One plus one is one. That is how musical memory works.
My cat almost died this week. He did not eat for four days
and slept a lot, and then he woke. He ate. He came back
from the end of the hall to be the silent music in our hands.

I want to write a song to honor the silence a song becomes.
In the middle, there will be a nothing, and, in the nothing,
someone small and misunderstood. And the music will hold
the listener the way a name holds a person without pretense
of capture. Music is merciful that way. And the long misread
will come to sing their praises as one. The end will come,
and all who listen will go silent. But a heartbeat continues
in the air they breathe, in the song of breathing no one hears.

Play a dissonance the first time, and it sounds uneasy,
needled with the feeling of something you forgot, some
name you misplaced, some error on the gravestone you
spend each midnight carving. But play it again, and you
hear a hint of pleasure, if not joy. It gives you permission,
room, a second wind. It opens a window, and a sky falls in.
Play it softer, deeper, and more tension falls away, like fire
from a star, and on and on, so long as you can take it.

How odd to come this far, from the body of another,
from the chain of strange and stranger bodies to the sea.
What I know of the cradle drifts into waves and pounds
the shore. If I meet infinity, I want to say, you and I are
not so different. I have heard your voice. I have drawn
the eye that drew me like a bow. Together we searched
each other's bodies. We emptied and filled. We said
you and I, you and I. We trembled like a telephone wire.

When I talk in my sleep, my cat turns to me to say, *Hey you in there, do you realize you are talking,* and so, I do, and so, I talk to my neighbor's wall. *Hey you in there, do you realize we can hear you,* and my cat thinks I am talking to her. *Hey,* she says, *without a bad connection, what good are dreams. What good are we without them. Why beat the mattress with our hearts, if not to pound a message to those too close, and far, and never there at all.*

No death for you. You are involved. So ends the poem
by a man whose car they found abandoned by a bridge.
No death certificate, no last note either, only the parting
glance in his opening line, the fading smiles of the bathers.
But even as the poem starts with departure, at least we know
our author was there, once, in the water. He gave it form
as bodies do. He immersed his trouble in the great Pacific,
if only as untouchable observer. So deep the peace that kills.

It took me one life to learn what I can live without.
It took me a life and one day after. Still I wonder.
The wandering of the desert fathers must have felt,
some days, a little pointless. But the one day after,
everything spoke. Every crystal burned with the call
of a castaway searching the sky. And then, it stopped.
Like talk at the table, when the house begins to shake,
when earth says what every silence whispers. I am here.

The one hand clapping at the end of the world is not alone.
It makes visible our only-ness. Then, it claps. It sounds
against the unspeakable like a boot against the streets of Berlin.
Some who survive say, we will always remember. We.
The museum with its hill of spectacles and shoes closes
for the evening, but the light is on. The swastika graffitied
on the door behind us shines. It will linger there a week
or so and then be painted over. We will never be alone.

Tonight, the role of the *abyss* will be played by clarinet,
as it was long ago, when Messiaen played it, when he filled
each breath at the opening with long tones and mourned
the killing fields of Europe. Before the trilling of the birds.
If this was the end of time, it possessed a force that kept on
singing to survive. A dialogue then, and fellow prisoners
at Görlitz heard it. It broke them in two. To hear a bird
take on the final burden. For an earth too beautiful to bear.

acknowledgments

The author would like to thank the editors of the *Common, Free Verse,* and the *Sewanee Review,* in which sections of this poem have appeared.

This volume is the forty-seventh recipient of the Juniper Prize for Poetry, established in 1975 by University of Massachusetts Press in collaboration with the UMass Amherst MFA program for Poets and Writers. The prize is named in honor of the poet Robert Francis (1901–1987), who for many years lived in Fort Juniper, a tiny home of his own construction, in Amherst.